cover photo: *It's also a chair*

cover lay out: Patrick Lebédeff
editor assistant: Stephan May

Special Thanks to: Alban Barré, Marianne Min-Denhard

© ÉDITIONS DIS VOIR, 2000
3, RUE BEAUTREILLIS
75004 PARIS

ISBN 2-906-571 95 4

PRINTED IN EUROPE

FRANÇOIS BAUCHET

this series edited by
PIERRE STAUDENMEYER

in the same series

FRANÇOIS BAUCHET

JACQUES BONNAVAL

CLAIRE FAYOLLE

CONTENTS

The simple story of a little chair

Design as One of the Fine Arts

*I*s it possible to say that a simple chair belongs to the realm of art? Intellectuals dismissed the very possibility long ago, with unquestioned authority. Yet it is precisely because that response is so spontaneous and unanimous that doubt, for me, creeps in. The absolutism of a received idea is never going to provide real answers; all it can do is short-circuit any inclination to ask questions. The many products of human endeavour have long since been exhaustively classified, with so-called taxonomic rigour. On the one hand, or so the theory goes, we have the pure emanations of the mind; on the other, everything that is subservient to the demands of strict necessity. It is thus possible to draw a totally reliable distinction between things that belong in the metaphysical domain and those that simply relate to the comfort of our behinds. The argument is irrefutable and what emerges from it is not just a classification but a value hierarchy, separating the products of immaculate thought from ordinary objects sullied by utilitarian concerns. Such hierarchies bear the characteristic stigmata of mysticism. They assume a split between mind and body, between eternal transcendence and the morbid curse of the here and now; the quarrel between the vileness of concrete things and the sublimity of the evanescent, between profane immediacy and sacred inaccessibility. Given, then, this irremediable divide, how can I claim without running the risk of heresy that a chair, which is basically just *there*, might somehow emanate from the very deepest regions of thought? How can we see it as anything other than an artificial extension of the supposedly inessential body? My intention is not to add yet more pages to this Byzantine discussion, in the service of which far too much ink has been spilt already. Though we should perhaps remember that the urge to mark out the boundaries of art as an autarchic (or should that perhaps be autistic?) domain is a relatively recent one. But what does all that matter since, when the time comes to look back, such trivial quarrels will vanish into the mists as works produced by the most diverse intentions and skills come together to chronicle the highest achievements of a spontaneous and nostalgic humanity. Is the humble potter of Mycenæ any less essential to our meditation than the *kouros* sculptor? Are the desks of the Medici Library mere wood without soul compared to the mind-rich incunabula resting upon them? And so on...

Such a large part of what we today consider to be our cultural heritage was never conceived with the specific intention of constituting a work of art in the sense of the word that intellectuals are now imposing on us. The arts and crafts jointly construct the signs on the basis of which a culture can develop and take off. In

It's also a chair (lacquered wood), 1981

my view, design today is attempting to bridge the gulf fostered by intellectual mysticism, creating an art which no longer sees itself as a doorway inviting escape into immaterial mental speculation, but is embodied instead in the simple making processes of existence, here and now, in the concreteness of the world, in the moment rescued from the brink of annihilation by the creative gesture. It is of course important to avoid any Manichaeism here. Design can also be an excuse for the direst duplicity, shamelessly selling out to the culture of frippery on which the universal consumerist spectacle gorges itself. Of course there are many designers who are nothing but third-rate illusionists, their reputations as short-lived as yesterday's fashion. But how could it be otherwise in these times when art is on the decline and anything can be called art so long as it has novelty value? I still like to believe that the best of humanity emerges through those products in which thought remains infinitely voluble amidst the chill silence of appearances.

These general observations come to mind as I think back over the career of François Bauchet. More than any other person, he forces me to wonder whether design is indeed one of the fine arts, or merely one of those subordinate types of production held in such disdain by the priesthood that promulgates our norms. Initially he was tempted by sculpture. In those distant (!) days he produced, as was more or less compulsory in all western art-schools at the time, works which generally adhered to conceptual and minimalist doctrines. However, as if taking a heretical stance towards those American minimalists for whom the laws of number and divination were one and the same thing (which made them idolatrous Pythagoreans), his work always retained a certain something, a vestigial sensory memory, which disrupted the rigidity of theoretical speculation. I believe that already for him at that time any shape, any line was the palimpsest of a lost sensation. It is as if, beneath the hegemony of appearances, there persisted an obsession with something repressed but essential. In this world of abstractions he needed to rediscover a concrete space in which thought might once again find it bearings and develop, not in deliberate neglect of reality, but by espousing it. Let there be design – and there was the *Little Chair*. I can no longer remember whether this *Little Chair* was indeed the first design object he created, but it stands out in my mind as the first fruit of his creative personality. Yes, for me the *Little Chair* is at once the outcome of all his earlier thinking and the starting-point of his work as a designer. It encapsulates everything out of which the later work would grow.

Even though this is a somewhat naïve way of looking at things, creative thinking might be said always to oscillate between two opposite temptations, one to exuberance, the other to asceticism. There is no doubt that François Bauchet is a man of strictly measured temperament and his *Little Chair* is above all a statement about simplicity. But such a straightforward claim should not make us miss some underlying key issues, for this is no mere stylistic preference for minimalism over mannerist extravagance. The important thing is the fundamental commitment governing Bauchet's choice, the kind of attitude which has been questioning the necessity and scope of western art since the distant beginnings of philosophical thought. Since truth can never been plural, says Plato, there can only be one accurate idea of what a bed (or any piece of furniture) truly is. This postulate implies that any concrete *realisation* of a bed necessarily involves a betrayal of some absolute original standard, and worse, that any *representation* of a bed further aggravates the drift away from an initial unity. It contains an implied condemnation of all artistic creation, a denial which has offered a constant temptation to speculative thinking through the ages. As is well known, only with Plotinus's dialectical reversal of this doctrine did it become possible to accept that, on the contrary, art is a process of idealising simplification in which the diversity of objects is reduced and the road to the absolute sketched out. For François Bauchet, the shift from sculpture to design was a way of incorporating the object's representation in its actual 'body'. Once an object has fused in this way with its own representation, it comes to designate its own underlying essence. This is not a matter of its necessity or its aesthetic meaning, but of the truth which it incarnates. The *Little Chair* is the epiphanic figure of that intention. For what does the *Little Chair* represent if not a temptation towards the Platonic archetype? It strives to achieve not merely an accurate adequation of form to function, but more importantly a fusion of the object (form as well as function) with the absolute simplification of the archetype. Nothing is more chair-like than this chair because what it makes present is the very idea 'chair'. While the billions of chairs scattered around the planet all refer to their own disparate singularity and anecdotal identity, pointing to signs of their history, the categories to which they belong, their originality, etc., the *Little Chair* stands out amid this prolix over-abundance in its negation of all distinctive, ornamental or anecdotal asperities, ultimately bringing us face to face with the bare presence of 'chair': that presence of the basic idea 'chair' in which appearances vanish to leave behind just a denotation. What governs this kind of intention is clearly a desire for the absolute. François Bauchet is trying to reach that point of fragile equilibrium where just one line added or taken away would forever veil the presence of the idea behind a curtain of narrative. The *Little Chair* is thus fundamentally the intuition of a paradox since, if it carries the aspiration for its concreteness to be sublimated in the non-materiality of the idea, that idea is thoroughly immanent in the chair itself; it is not manifest somewhere outside the chair, but rather attains its plenitude through it. The idea and its concrete expression completely co-exist. Through its symbiosis between simplicity and self-evidence the *Little Chair* gives modest expression to François Bauchet's firmly-held convictions. The lacquered monochrome finish inscribes an erasure, veiling structural complexity behind a unified surface appearance. The particularities of the materials used and the vagaries of their assembly disappear, allowing the pure form to shine out in its minimal totality. Function and ideal blend together in a presence which nothing can spoil. In profile, all that can be seen are the one horizontal and two vertical lines of the ordinary chair. The original chair. Just the archetype, in which the material and the mental have yet to be separated. In profile, an 'h'; the 'h' in the word 'chair'; the initial 'h' of *humanitas, homo, humanus.* Signs have a strange status because what creates presence in them is what is fundamentally absent. As will by now be clear, the *Little Chair* is at once a totality and the sign of a lack. Its isolation designates it as forever orphaned of being. What is lacking is the other side of the object/human pairing. What is missing is the person whom the seat is designed to

Vanity (lacquered wood), 1981

accommodate: the 'h' of the person sitting down so as to create a desired primordial unity with the 'h' of the chair. The chair in its isolation is but the *sombra del hombre*. Various of François Bauchet's commentators, most notably Hervé Audouard, have stressed this presence of absence. The way in which all formal or decorative affectation is stripped away further reinforces this poignant truth. His reduction of the object to its silhouette, to the nudity of an elementary sign, is part of the dramaturgy of a missing presence. However total it may seem to be, the object only has meaning in relation to human concerns. Is this meaning just a simple relationship to the body, as is generally assumed? Is the object just a prosthesis? Is a chair just an instrument to allow *Homo Erectus* to avoid collapsing on the ground as soon as his legs start to wilt? That may well be generally true, but what François Bauchet points out is that form is not just something induced by bodily necessity: it actually designates the whole of being. The object is not content simply to suggest an absence, it invites us to ponder the fundamental being of that absent other. It encourages us to perceive that which is missing.

To illustrate my point, let us look briefly at what François Bauchet himself has called his *addressed pieces*. These were created in the years immediately following the *Little Chair*. At first sight it is not even absolutely clear that they are furniture items at all: their function is far from obvious, and they are indeed strange, singular objects. In comparison with the extreme stylisation of the *Little Chair*, they have something odd about them. When you see them you feel rather as you do when, on a visit to a museum of lost civilisations, you are confronted by objects whose basic use is completely unfamiliar: you guess what they are for, rather than fully understanding. One is called *to P. F (Writing Case in Lacquered Wood)*, another *to D.L. (Lectern in Lacquered Wood)*. Such titles are obviously valuable clues to the identity of these objects, but in a sense the need to interpret them only deepens the mystery. Our questions skirt around them without finding even the smallest certainty to cling to. These figures seem totally unpredictable in comparison to the ordinary inventory of design. They are all the stranger for the fact that they achieve their effect in the geometrical sobriety of a shape whose lacquered monochrome mass makes it impenetrable to the gaze. In fact, it is as if these were ritual objects carved from the lacquered mass and dedicated to who knows what divinities. They are not utilitarian but religious objects. Of course anyone who knows the circles in which François Bauchet moves can work out the clues contained in a title such as *to P. F (Writing Case in Lacquered Wood)*: the dedication to a certain P.F., whose life and work are confined inside the walls of a *scriptorium*. For those who know the identity of this mischievous bookworm ceaselessly scribbling away at his miniatures within the encircling fold of his arm (like a secretive schoolboy, his mind far removed from the maths lesson, concealing his escapist misdemeanours), the writing case speaks of an encounter with the hieroglyphs of the imagination, a work in which the miniscule opens up a secret doorway onto adolescent escape. Looking next at the lectern called *to D.L.*, we realise at once that it is dedicated to an artist whose way of working and upright stance are radically opposed to P. F's. While one evokes the seated roundness of posture, a hunching concentration into the miniaturist's gesture, the other on the contrary speaks of the painter's state of hieratic contemplation before his inscrutable canvas: no question here of sitting, the lectern hardly more than a prop to a verticality unbowed by the slightest doubt. These two *addressed pieces* (to P.F. and D.L.) are not just inspired by different working postures, they are metaphorical portraits of two opposing artistic personalities. The addressed pieces designate and differentiate them just as surely as a humble straw-seated chair expresses the solitary despair of Van Gogh, or a throne emblazoned with coats of arms evokes ebullient power. In these two works François Bauchet is demonstrating how function cannot simply be reduced to functionalism; how form is not simply a matter of formalism; how an object is the sign of a singularity or a culture which always need to be decoded beneath the veil of its all-too obvious appearance. In order to be fully aware of the mystery of these objects we need to proceed exactly as we would when faced with the enigmatic creations of another civilisation: we have to ask ourselves to which divinity they are sacred. That is exactly what I was doing earlier when I suggested that the *Little Chair* was *la sombra del hombre ausente*.

As I have already mentioned, all through the 1980s unified colour absorbed disparities in construction, while the work process went to extreme lengths to conceal itself. There is here a classical ethos according to which the work of art must not betray anything of its origin in the couplings of sweat and the hammer, or the intellectual labour of its creator, but rather present an immaculate exterior from which questions can take flight without the least hindrance from formal difficulties. The work as absolute presence. Not only did François Bauchet renounce all embellishment in favour of a pared-down monochrome, he also abandoned any singularity of style or aim for originality in order that the work be nothing but itself in all its naked presence; that this presence be nothing but the enigma of itself as presence. I have no doubt that the onlooker in a hurry (as modern life forces everyone to be) will regard what I am saying as complete nonsense and wonder why I am talking about enigmas when there is nothing the slightest bit enigmatic about a chair reduced to its simplest expression. But since I have this text to write, I for one have to take the time to pause before the things which offer themselves to my contemplation. In any case, why does this chair draw my gaze so powerfully when all the asperities of signs have been erased from it, when its colouring is discretion itself, etc.? What is it that makes this chair into an emblem of chairs and not just something to sit on? Something about it intrigues me, and that something is the fact that it is just a little bit smaller than an ordinary chair. It is this tiny detail, this almost unnoticed something less, that allows it to command more attention. It is this barely perceived lack that encourages us not just to look at it as an object for sitting on, but to meditate on what it is that makes it such an accurate designation of human identity. By means of this small lack, François Bauchet invites us to progress from our unconsidered usage of an object to taking the time to contemplate it.

Lack and Loss

Let me stress again that assertion by erasure is one of the essential characteristics of François Bauchet's work, at a time when didacticism, exaggerated effects, playing with chance, the systematic disruption of expectations, etc. are becoming both the means and the end for most people who have creative ambitions; when any anecdotal extravagance is liable to be celebrated as a discovery of genius. In this context, the things generally regarded as 'works' with important 'signatures' are those which exhibit their determination to be original for originality's sake. People will buy a coffee pot which carries the name of some famous architect even if, *as* a coffee pot, it is of very limited use. That does not matter since in this case what is being bought is not the coffee pot as such, but the formal embellishments on it which serve to identify the architect. All superficial cultures end up by only being interested in appearances and so turn themselves into a sham. François Bauchet is utterly indifferent to the busy exhibitionism of his contemporaries. For him, the craft of design is not about exaggerating one's anecdotal creative singularity, or indeed the work/materials dialectic: it is a matter of achieving complete mastery, striving towards the ultimate point where all trace of craft itself disappears. In accordance with this classical ambition, all the different phases of design and execution disappear into the unitary opacity of the lacquered mass. It might be imagined that this use of lacquer is purely skin deep, only there for its ability to cover over any problems with materials or assembly, or because it adds an aesthetically-pleasing veil of colour; but the lacquer emerges from its own concealment. There is not the slightest juxtaposition of colour for visual effect. No bright tones attract the gaze. Colour never makes any aesthetic claims for itself, nor strives to single out the object. It is anonymous. It is a coloured material in which the colour itself seems to have been completely absorbed (a camouflage green which camouflages itself *as* green; a brown in which the red tones fail to stand out; a grey in which the light scarcely emerges from the dark, etc. Always the same discretion in the shadow of the primary colours). Dull colours which any attempt to define simply pushes deeper down into the impossibility of naming. Everyone tries to describe the colour of that 'skin', so like a real epidermis, yet no suitable word comes to mind. It is a colour in which all others are hidden. It is what covers things over and brings unity to what is diverse and separate. It is that concealment which paradoxically confers on the body its full alterity.

The work of François Bauchet cannot be understood without taking this aspect into account. Anyone who is content just to analyse the materials and techniques he uses, and the history, context and function etc. of his works, will completely miss his intentions and therefore the profound reality of the objects that he offers to our gaze. He has a longing for absolute immanence (which is a paradox in view of the usual dichotomy between immanence and the absolute). In order to achieve this, the object must be, at one and the same time, both erasure and presence. It is by erasing its modes of conception and production that the work asserts its irrefutable presence. A work born out of a labour in which its creator erases himself is condemned to a solitary fate. This next statement might seem incongruous to anyone who clings to the idea that objects only have reality if they are regarded as accessories (as soon as you look at them in isolation, such objects seem forever to be lacking a human counterpart), but it is clear to

Good morning Mr..., writing desk and *Drums* seat (lacquered wood), 1984

me that a creation like the *Little Chair* offers itself to us as sufficient unto itself, just like any other authentic work of art. Doubtless its predicate 'chair' presupposes the complement 'human', but who would claim that people's everyday wish is to sit on an archetype? On the contrary, all the evidence is that the everyday need to have something to sit on entails a constant drift of seating further and further away from its archetype. Who would claim that the archetype is the primary datum of usage? There is no need to contemplate the *Little Chair* at length to realise that it is an image of the fundamental chair, without that making its usage value into its most essential characteristic. It is the most paradoxical of objects, at one and the same time the most chair-like of chairs, yet one that asks to be contemplated rather than sat on.

Until now I have called it the *Little Chair*, but that is only because the general points I wanted to make required such a neutral designation. In fact, the name François Bauchet gave it is quite different: he called it *This is Also a Chair*. This entirely confirms the point of view that I have been developing hitherto. The real name indicates that this is not from its inception a chair on which certain aesthetic qualities have conferred the status of a design object, but rather that what we have here is an object of some sort or other which might in the end be regarded as a chair. In the same way, the Pharaoh's throne was originally a designation of his divine election, and only secondarily a seat. The deliberately-chosen title points out that the object is not just an object. Not just an object? Like Magritte's famous picture *This is Not a Pipe*, it proclaims its status, somewhat tautologically, as a representation or designation of an object. The title *This is Also a*

Chair announces that its essence is not reducible to appearances or usage. Only secondarily a statement of function (as with Van Gogh's chair in the Arles bedroom), it suggests that the chair is telling us something fundamental, something that governs entirely the fate of an absent being. Using Heideggerian terminology (despite my general misgivings about German philosophy and its unwieldy concepts), one might say that something of the order of truth is at work within the work. But what is that something given that truth itself, which can always only be sensed, is an impossible finitude? A truth of the chair? Or of design? Both of those, or something different? Something more obvious yet impossible to reduce to a statement?

The power of a work of art lies of course in its ability to bring us face to face with ourselves. Its objective is to reveal to us the hidden but obvious reality of existence. What is made manifest through it is the fundamental humanity of our condition. But in the case of the *Little Chair* we can but admit that the human has all the appearance of a disappearing act. I have even suggested already that there is actually a double disappearance here: the vanishing creator, sublimated in his craft, and the absence of any human complement for the object. The object for sitting on signals the lack of a person to do so and it is this presence of an absence which inevitably stimulates our urge to question. But what would be the point of wondering about the singular identity of the *hombre ausente*, except as a way of peopling our individual fantasies? What would be the point of setting out in quest of a particular type of being, since by choosing to confront us with the *arkhetupon*, François Bauchet is bringing us face to face not with a specific chair but with the idea 'chair', whatever its circumstantial variations and historical developments may be? By setting before us an archetype, he is referring us to the general notion of fundamental being. The missing figure with which we are involved here, which captures our entire attention by taking on the status of an enigma, is paradoxically given by the evident human allusion. The missing person is quite simply Man. Of course we could invent pretty well any sort of story, but there is no affectation of form, no explicit sign to hint at a specific situation or provide the starting-point for any sort of narrative.

All possible interpretations remain open, but no particular imaginative pathway is privileged. What does the *Little Chair* teach us about Humanity if not that we are human? That we are *Homo Erectus* (a posture which establishes the gap between us and the animal kingdom) and as such we feel the need to sit down! We could admittedly follow the example of the bare-bottomed baboons in the zoo and sit with our behinds on the ground. But we are also *Homo Faber* with the ability to imagine an artificial extension for our bodies which will keep our buttocks off the rough stones. But that in turn comes down to saying that we are *Homo Sapiens*, designers of the object 'chair'. Being all of these at once makes us in fact cultural beings: in other words, we see the artefact designed to keep our buttocks off the ground not just as a functional appendage of our lumbar region, but as an object which gradually begins to accrete the layered signs which are the foundation of our history. How does the *Little Chair* express all that? It actually says nothing: it just *is*. But, isolated in the extreme sparseness of its imaginative origins, it invites a contemplation in which the hidden reality suddenly reveals itself. This digression on the development of human ingenuity would be merely a naive truism if there were not, right at the secret heart of the work, some essential statement about the tragic destiny of humanity. Something that remains unsaid, yet that everything suggests. Something that goes beyond the mere progression from behind on the ground to comfortable chair. To pursue Heideggerian terminology, whatever illusory triumphs we may achieve, we remain squeezed in the dialectic between the earth and the will, and it is in that forever unresolved conflict that mankind is condemned to locate its ephemeral moments of enlightenment. If the will of man as an upright being is indeed to erect an ever-higher world (one in keeping at once with his image and with his dreams), if he always speaks of elevation, etc., his only certain destiny nevertheless remains in the bowels of the earth. The strict verticality of the chair back points to man as a haughty being sustained by his culture in a constant yearning for elevation, an elevation which is also of the very essence in the psychic make-up of *Homo Erectus*. His single obsession is with this erect posture which he imagines will allow him to escape a morbid fate. However, the implacable terrestrial gravity that shackles any illusion of escaping into absolute elevation also constrains him to sit down. His mind soars, his body remains heavy. The *Little Chair* is an outstanding illustration of this constraining paradox of being. The dialectics of our being are expressed in two lines. The vertical rises towards an escape from our primordial condition, while, at right angles to the back, the horizontal on which the body rests its weight stands as a reminder of the implacability of a destiny in which all life is but a striving for the impossible. The chair designates man as the thinking (and therefore making) being who rises above his original animality but remains bound by the earthly fate of his body.

There can be no simpler statement than this simple little chair of the dialectic between elevation and gravity that underlies the whole of existence. No clearer statement of the dialectic between splendour and poverty in the ephemeral glimmer of our thought, always thirsting for fresh illusions. So here it is, that absent persona suddenly made present, the one to whose sublime aspiration within a tragic destiny the *Little Chair* bears witness. The *Little Chair* speaks to us not about chairs, but about the very foundations of our existence. Yes, that is what the *Little Chair* is saying with its elegant, changeless stature and haughty posture in search of the absolute, yet which its heavy body installs in the inexorable grip of gravity. People will naturally object that what I am saying is just a collection of truisms and that the same could be said of any other chair. Of course, but what we need to remember is that ever since chairs were chairs, their designers, through their preoccupation with symbolic or straightforwardly decorative additions, with singularity and originality at any price, and with stressing their own skill etc., have constantly diverted people's attention towards visual (functional or socio-cultural) connotations, making it no longer possible to perceive a chair *as* simply a chair. Circumstantial appearances have ended up by masking the original basis on which the chair expressed man in his very being, before he became obsessed with the pleasure of possessing objects. François Bauchet's *Little Chair* is neither a kitchen chair nor a living-room one, a boudoir chair, a decorated chair or one laden with social signs, or even one displaying the effects of design: it is a chair archetype whose essentials are completely open to view. Nothing of what we see of it depends on futile superstructures, everything resides in its simple chair body. Saying *This is Also a Chair* presupposes that it is above all a questioning of the notion of chair in its naked presence, and that the metaphysical statement is to be found in its archetype memory: it is in the co-existence of the chair's 'h' shape and the 'h' in *humanitas* that the metaphysical statement is at once concealed and offered to our meditation. The super-abundance of eclectic chairs throughout our consumer societies shows us man in his desire to have, whereas the archetype shows him in his fundamental being, normally masked to an ever-increasing degree by the blur of appearances. It then becomes fairly obvious that the question of which attributes of craftsmanship, narrative, or aesthetics etc., distinguish the artistic artisan from the pure artist, is verging on the point of total entropy. What makes François Bauchet a properly artistic creator, rather then just a producer of objects, is the anxiety over essentials that he carries inside himself: the important thing is not form in itself, but the fact that through the immanence of form some fundamental truth is offered to our meditation. 'Truth only unfolds its being as a battle between enlightenment and reserve, in the conflict between worldly aspiration and the earth', wrote Heidegger. We should note that this desire to grasp a fundamental reality is precisely what the sophistication of anecdotal or socio-cultural appearances is determined to block. Any human culture in a position to enjoy

To Denis L. (lacquered wood), 1986

having will deliberately seek to block off *being*. Here too we find a fundamental truth: a form of knowledge has developed which enforces an ignorance of being. François Bauchet's task is to be an archaeologist digging down through layers of cultural trivia, going back in time through a plethora of formal deposits to uncover the lone archetype not yet rendered unreadable by the excess of signs. The *Little Chair* is a statement of the founding paradoxes out of which emerge the road towards a conquest which is also a denial.

Ascesis and Meditation

I am aware that, despite this statement, most observers will see in the *Little Chair* only a chair made of lacquered wood. Equally, they will obviously only see in 'The Legend of the True Cross' by Pierro della Francesca a man staggering along with a T-shaped wooden object over his shoulder. If something else is to speak to them, something not immediately perceptible, they will need to take the time to ask themselves questions, and give the work time to make the scales fall from their eyes. But in an age when people think they know it all, they no longer feel any need to come towards the work and meet it on its own terms, they regard it as just a part of the scenery which they see without really seeing it. For my part, I aim to suspend the glancing drift of our gaze, to allow prolixity to arise from an object of discretion, and speech to well up from the silence of things. But for that to happen, we need to be capable of adopting an ascetic turn of mind. This involves a necessary loss, which François Bauchet invites us to accept. The *arkhetupon* does not just have the value of primordial universality: it *is* the original renunciation. The *Little Chair* is an allegory of all ascetic aspirations. It would be wrong to see ascesis in this context as involving solely the virtues of self-mortification or the rejection of temporal delights; it is also about a free-flowing spiritual pleasure (I use the term spiritual here in the sense of psychic activity). It is a moment when contemplation of an ordinary presence leads to the appearance of something extraordinary. Let me stress the fact that the quest for a forgotten *arkhetupon* is above all a path of renunciation. It is by renouncing all the circumstantial vanities of appearance that François Bauchet is able to rediscover not just the simple form but also the essence of the object. He exhumes from beneath the accumulated strata of appearances the initial numinous figure of the created object. Craftsmanship here succeeds in erasing all trace of itself, arriving at a form devoid of all decorative embellishments so that, in the end, the onlooker is relieved of any need to pay attention to the chair's material corporeality, and can concentrate instead on the concept 'chair'. In other words, instead of the object capturing his or her attention through some novel idea, it induces thoughts about its essential nature. Once the point is reached where form and *conceto* become coexistent in the numinous presence of an archetypal figure, transcendence and immanence become one. It is in the object's pure presence that something inscribed within it becomes available to be released.

I remember a story which is told by the Little Sisters of the Revelation in Nazareth. Intrigued by the anchoritic behaviour of Charles de Foucauld, they sent one of their number on a mission to visit this new *poverello* in his hut. The nun reported that there was

nothing but a stone to sit on and a plank by way of a desk. When they talk about asceticism the Little Sisters refer only to furniture, nothing else. It is as if they regarded it as self-evident that furniture is the most accurate measure of man and that therefore, spiritual ascesis goes hand in hand with a minimum of furniture. This anecdote (one of many that I could have quoted, but it is particularly pleasing that it relates to the Little Sisters of the Revelation) tells us that furniture is the eloquent allegory of our being. The *Little Chair* shows how concerned François Bauchet is to stimulate being-related thoughts about the chair, both as its creator (thinking verticality) and as someone who needs to sit down (unavoidable gravity). It is a *mode of being* rather than a *way of having* that governs his creative thinking. The primary thing for him is his ethical aspiration, which underpins his whole aesthetic with a denial of aestheticism. Being is the essence which needs to be rediscovered beneath the omnipotence of form and formalism.

I would perhaps not be so confident in making these claims were there not other works, subsequent to the *Little Chair*, that confirm what I am saying much more explicitly. I am thinking in particular of the *Coiffeuse* (Dressing-Table), although I do not remember exactly in which year it was made (shortly after the *Little Chair*, I think). What is immediately striking is the shape, which is like a three-panelled altar-piece, or *retable*; with all the sobriety of the archetypal altar-piece. Monochrome grey, the kind that seems to absorb all colour. At first glance there is nothing more simply or more obviously functional than this piece of furniture. So it appears, but long acquaintance with François Bauchet's creations has taught me that appearances are but the veil of an immanence that demands to be espoused by a questioning gaze. This is an piece of furniture in front of which a young woman devotes herself to the alchemy of her own metamorphosis. It is a kind of test by mask, a mask of makeup which covers up the age of the face, perhaps, but also a mask of playful seduction, one of consensual beauty concealing unlovely singularity, of powders and potions smoothing out little details and disparities, etc. This transfiguration ritual is after all nothing more than a young woman's everyday experience, a heritage of the earliest cultures. What could be more natural and anodyne than this innocent activity? What could be more normal? So why bother with convoluted questions on this point, even without loading them with inappropriate moral connotations?

Yet, what I cannot help but find troubling here is the fact that François Bauchet takes a view of the dressing-table diametrically opposed to the one which has evolved throughout the course of history. The very notion of a dressing-table itself has become a symbol of feminine adornment. All its signs point in one way or another to a ritual of sophistication, seduction or frivolity, of attention to non-serious things. Dressing-tables are weighed down with allegorical ornaments, whether they be explicitly figured or merely suggested by pastel colours, convoluted carvings or precocity of manner. Dressing-tables in a sense set up a theatrical décor within which the woman plays the role of *femme fatale*. Bauchet's *Coiffeuse* does none of that. It has the austerity of an altar-piece triptych in which nothing is shown, either figuratively or symbolically, through curvaceous arabesques or the evanescence of coloured backgrounds. It is simply a triptych in which colour

A/rangement 1 (lacquered wood), 1982

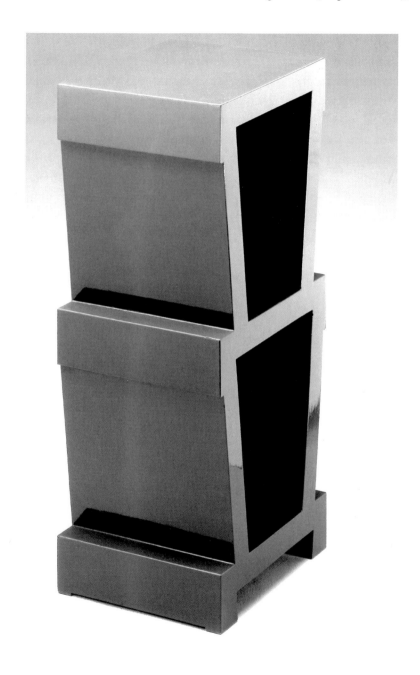

itself is in some way an evaporation of colour; this plain piece of furniture in no way suggests itself as an altar at which some priestess might officiate in the service of discord. No-one would think of suggesting as much because nothing disturbs the earnest serenity of this *sanctum*. Why not indeed speak of it as a sanctuary, since when the austere structure is examined in its bare presence, it is clearly a retable which has yet to be complemented by its pictorial predella. Thus here again, as when looking at the *Little Chair*, we find ourselves haunted by a lack. What is obviously absent is the allegorical ceremony that is culturally indissociable from feminine adornment, which in a sense represents a fantasy looking-glass world. Bauchet, like a Cistercian battling against the Benedictines of Cluny, has stripped this consecrated space bare of all frivolity that might disturb our pure contemplation. He is telling us without beating about the bush that beyond fictitious ceremonial, beyond naive symbolism, beyond the fictional drama played out in the theatre of appearances, etc., we ought to wonder about the deeper meaning of this ritual in which self-exhibition actually serves a desire for concealment. It is paradoxically by taking away all signs of frivolity that he invites us to wonder what is going on in this frivolous ritual played out in front of the mirror, that icon *par excellence*. His choice of an altar-piece as model only increases the urgency of this invitation to meditation.

My purpose here is obviously not to indulge in an endless disquisition on women's makeup rituals. I could go back over their devotion to beauty, men, love, sensuality, inaccessibility, metempsychosis, etc., all at the same time and much else besides, and that would be all the more relevant as the dressing-table has become, in both our everyday imagination and in literature, the symbolic attribute of the tart. But Bauchet has erased all of that to induce a sense of enigma and to make absence even more obsessively present. All I can say is that in the sanctuary of the retable, such a pared-down exterior forces us into a face-to-face encounter with the only icon there is – the mirror. If the mirror is indeed an icon, it can only be an icon to vanity. 'Mirror, mirror in the wall, tell me who I am'; yet we all know that in the fairy-tale what that really means is: 'Tell me I am the woman I want to be, not who I really am.' While she is at her makeup a young woman believes that mask-like other to be Herself. In the course of the ceremony, what the woman sitting at the dressing-table passionately requires it to display is not her reality, but rather its concealment by disguise: what she wishes to offer to the gaze of the other is the un-truth of her adornment, not her reality. Of course, this ritual cannot be reduced to some religious fear of appearances, but the symbolic language underlying seduction is composed of the convoluted signs of a delusion which taints all lucidity. It may be objected that I am again straying a long way from François Bauchet's actual creations and becoming bogged down in so many different considerations that any sense of a clear statement is swamped; that I am drifting off the point and discussing almost everything except design. However, the patient reader who is mindful of my opening arguments and has not forgotten my contention that François Bauchet is a creator of true works of art, not just functional or aestheticising objects, will appreciate that these works are not only open to constant re-interpretation, they are also concerned with the essential but concealed reality of human existence. As with the *Little Chair*, in the *Coiffeuse* we see played out before our eyes not the simple business of appearances, but the whole inexorable tragedy of being: the short-lived illusion of being able to flee from our implacable fate.

In a similar way to the *Little Chair*, the *Coiffeuse* might have been called *This is Also a Dressing Table,* since its only function is to designate that which we fundamentally are, and because, through the gradual cultural dulling of our responses, we have grown used to regarding as a superficial *somatic* phenomenon what is really a pure emanation of the *psyche.* The world of objects belongs to the species that thinks, and to it alone. Objects are in no way reducible to mere prosthetic attempts to satisfy our bodily needs. To put it another way, they bear witness to a metaphysical anxiety whose epic story is inscribed symbolically in the skills developed to make them, not just to a list of logical features intrinsic in those skills. We should remember that aspects of Pythagoras that we nowadays regard as being about the objective measurement of concrete reality in fact originated from a central ontological anxiety in the Tetrachtys. By selecting the *Coiffeuse*, François Bauchet has decided to present us with something that undeniably derives from functional skills, but is designed to perform a purely cultural ritual. It goes without saying that I am using the word 'cultural' in a sense which is a legacy of religious ontological anxiety. Even if in this case it is extremely difficult to distinguish the sacred from the profane, the fact that he has opted for the allegorical figure of the alter-piece only confirms what I have been saying. This piece of furniture displays perfect syncretism between the *cultural* and the *devotional.* It introduces frivolity into the original sphere of the religious, speaking to us about what makes them different and what they have in common.

However, what common ground can there be between the young woman at her dressing-table and the worshipper dumbstruck with piety before the icon of a retable? What might be their shared quest? It seems clear that each is in search of the truth about themselves, even if in one case that truth takes the form of a message about appearances and in the other an invisible secret. The identical thing is that in each the desire for revelation is at the same time a rejection of reality. The young woman wants to discover herself in her adorned other in the same way as the worshipper wants to convince himself that his is an immortal destiny, not just a short-lived passage on Earth. Each is striving to exorcise time, which has made them while simultaneously undoing them. Neither the coquette's mirror nor the sublime icon is designed to show what is, but rather to develop the fictions of desire. In both cases the specular image is but a reversal of reality. The apparent quest is for the construction of an imaginary double, in other words it testifies to the impossibility of our ever facing what we are: reality cannot be fully assumed, wrote Lacan. Thinking is basically a constant attempt to escape from the real world. Whether kneeling before the icon in the hope of receiving grace or sitting in front of the mirror trying to avoid disgrace, the prayer is the same; the same desperate hope of being different from the way we are. And it is precisely thanks to this desperate hope, this originating thought, that all the world's religions, philosophies, ideologies and cultures, all the infinite number of petty preoccupations that cast an illusory halo of meaning around our

Hopper (punched steel), 1982

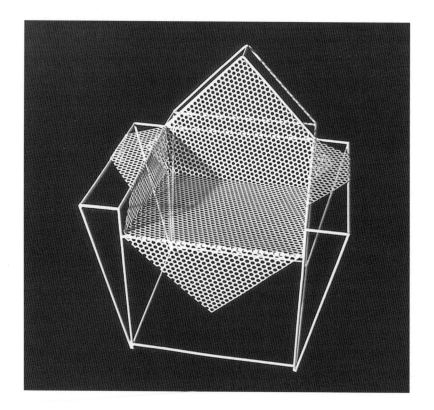

fleeting hours and days, are able indefinitely to perpetuate themselves into the future. Like the *Little Chair*, the *Coiffeuse* speaks of the paradoxical condition of being. Although this is an over-simplification, it could be said that in the *Little Chair* François Bauchet was referring to *Homo Erectus* in his dichotomy between elevation and heaviness, while in the Retable-*Coiffeuse* he is pointing to *Homo Sapiens* faced with the insoluble contradiction between his desire to know and his rejection of knowledge; or in other words, the fact that thought is unavoidably a magic veil cast over a too-obvious reality. In both works he reveals the foundations of the tragedy of being for all thinking organisms.

Any reader persistent enough to have followed my meandering digression to the end should now be persuaded that François Bauchet is not just any old furniture maker but a creator of highly emblematic works. To use a slightly excessive image, I would say that for him the design of an object can no more be reduced to its immediate function than the Saqqarah Pyramid was in the mind of Imoteph just a place of rest for the departed body. All the time, the pared-down lines of the object evoke the inscrutable depths of the psyche. If the reader will bear with me a while longer in considering the *Coiffeuse*, once we realise that surface adornment in fact conceals an implacable reality, it becomes obvious that the ascetic barrenness of the retable (in which Giotto's ever so pure Madonna has vanished into herself) refers by subtraction to the fact that our history of forms seeking ever-new visual affectations simply covers up the objects' original power of communication beneath the disguise of their aspectual exhibitionism. It takes a Baudelaire sick with lucidity to realise that a divan can be as deep as a tomb. Is formal ostentation anything more than concealment? Does ornamentation do anything other than cover up what is essential? Is the devotion to appearances anything but a diversion for a gaze that has become blind to fundamentals? Is it not an acceptance of superficial flattery in place of an austerity of conscience? Is the dramatising of appearances not similar in all respects to the artifice of makeup, which aims to turn our gaze on reality into an impossible gaze? Is this not the definitive triumph of an exhibition culture over a culture concerned with modes of being? The triumph of *having* over *existing*? A refusal to see that the important part in any object is what goes on inside us? That is certainly the most Cistercian aspect of François Bauchet, expressed in the bareness of forms reduced to their most fundamental numbers. The austerity of the *Coiffeuse* reduced to the retable archetype (in other words, its designation by what is lacking) points up a double concealment perpetrated first by interior designers, then by designers of furniture: concealment of the necessary behind a veil of seduction, and concealment of our original relationship to the object. It seems that with the gradual spread of manufactured and industrial production, designers became obsessed with demonstrating their skill to the detriment of all fundamentals. The exhibitionism of designers who reduced objects to their own stylistic prowess implies a world in which appearances are the ultimate goal.

There are other examples in François Bauchet's output which confirm his intuition that there is a metaphysical presence immanent in all things, an intuition which haunts the whole of his work. I will just say a few words about his famous bed (thereby

Liliploon chair (fiberglass), 1985

leaving every reader free to meditate on it further for themselves). This is an object that has often been criticised for being over-emphatic, and regarded as deviant in relation to the rule of austerity that he imposed on himself from the beginning. These criticisms are only valid if the bed is considered solely from the formal point of view and if, in fact, one accepts the premise that formalism is the supreme goal of any creative act. However, given that in his work form always ultimately co-exists with a (meditated, not pre-meditated) idea, the bed's imposing majesty is there to signify his exuberance at life's unpredictability. This is not just a simple space in which to sleep in comfort, but one in which the whole epic story of being is played out, from its alpha to its omega. It is the place of birth, of death, of rest from fatigue, of ordinary copulation and sumptuous orgy; the place of sleepless nights and consummated unions, pleasure and grief, ecstasy amid terror; the place where life seeks a refuge from life and yet comes face to face with itself. A fortress in which to dream of El Dorado, yet a toy castle besieged on all sides by fate. A place in which the profane surges up from mysterious depths. A Holy of Holies which night constantly condemns us to inhabit.

Ascesis is immanent to each of François Bauchet's objects, whose pared-down form is contained within minimal lines and whose colouration contains all colours to the point of un-namability. Ascesis is actually what compels us to renounce the received wisdom according to which the only pleasure we can derive from our relationships with objects comes from the socio-cultural recognition of ownership and the comfort of usage. As a result of this minimalism achieved by removing all attractive colours, emphatic symbolism, distracting mannerisms, the slightest sign in which the seed of a narrative might grow, our gaze, not encouraged to drift away into diversions or hypnotised by artifice, finds itself held in the trap of pure contemplation. And we can be sure that what François Bauchet hopes to achieve by inviting us to risk this kind of meditation is to remind us that any mode of production that does not consider man simply in terms of a producer/consumer duality remains implicated in a field of metaphysics which we must never accept as being obsolete (is this not a way of reconnecting ourselves with the potter of Mycenæ?). This does not just mean that it is still possible to work outside the mainstream consumerist spectacle (an expression that I use here in its pure situationist sense), it is also a matter of wondering, as Hölderlin did, where the temptation comes from to create (to produce open works) in these days of stagnation when people readily take comfort in the pretty-pretty. François Bauchet stands aside from the sound and fury generated by the exuberant and proliferating manifestations of his contemporaries, for he knows that new thinking does not come from signing up to everyone else's logic and accepting the hegemony of received ideas, but rather originates in the haven of a meditative distance from them. Any genuine intellectual process presupposes a constant willingness to take risks in thinking; to test thought against life and life against thought; to think that the question will remain forever questioning, and not put to sleep our ontological anxiety. Once this is understood it should come as no surprise to learn that François Bauchet has designed an artists' residence organised along monastic lines. While this certainly implies an ethical point of view, it is one quite unconnected with of orthodox mystical fervour; his own fervent belief is that it is not enough for a creator simply to keep turning out things that are already known, he or she must constantly ponder the essential questions. So I can well believe that the monastic furniture that he has designed for the artists in residence is a little joke based on his reasons for refusing to take part in the world of so-called modern art: an invitation to them to ponder their fate. But that is another story, and for all 'incurable handymen' that type of meditation will always remain *terra incognita*.

In the inventory of works produced by François Bauchet in the course of the 1980s there are many other pieces which originated in the same humanistic inspiration. One that comes to mind, for example, is a desk called *Men in Uniform*. Once again, it is the archetypal desk: two lateral supports and a top, at once the simplest and most obvious of desks. *This is a Desk*. No words could better state its self-evidence. Nothing could be added to it without detracting from its unitary perfection. This time it is not a portrait of an individual but an allegory of a whole social group (not just any old group, but the one whose austere mode of being has remained virtually unchanged since the days of the most ancient legions). The strict rigour of the object testifies to the behavioural rigidity of its human complement. This desk's austere presence is not content to say that someone is absent (that un-named person who fills our imagination with their effusions): it names the absent *Man in Uniform* whose ethic precisely consists in renouncing his own individual being.

Installation of the Cartier Foundation, 1985

I now need to bring this slightly confused little text, more enthusiastic than rigorous, to a conclusion. While I was writing these pages and fumbling for words, François Bauchet was in Vallauris making a series of ceramic objects for the table; very beautiful objects which seem almost haloed in the purity of their curves. I have only seen a few pictures of them in magazines. The one that has remained imprinted in my mind is the last of the series, a sort of large amphora with stylised curves, like the women of Mycenæ or black Africa. An amphora for wine, oil, the elixir of love... how should I know? It is an astonishingly modern amphora and yet it seems to have been raised from a galleon long since swallowed up in the memory of the deep, while on the surface of history the super-abundance of forms went on lining up its cortege of ephemera. An amphora in which some potion of knowledge still gives off an unspeakable magic.

The framework of life

You have a sculptor's training. The work of the Support/-Surface group and the American minimalists, especially Donald Judd and Sol Lewitt, have been a determining factor for you during the 1970s. Entering your thirties, how did that shift from one practice to another, from art to design, happen?

I was born into a family of architects and from an early age was interested in objects, to such an extent that I even considered entering the Ecole Nationale Supérieure des Arts décoratifs. But, on my first visit there, it seemed to me that their projects were completely rigid. The only certainty I had at the time was to feel some concern for the process of creation, for the framework of my life, and the framework of life. I sensed that art as well as architecture had a role to play. But I didn't have any architectural ambition as I was too close to the reality of that profession. It's through reaction to the system that I preferred a framework that recognized more freedom of expression, and freedom of thought. Thanks to that orientation I was able to meet painters and sculptors. In reality I was as much interested in the rivalry created

by the exchanges between artists than in the works themselves. It seemed to me that it was no longer possible to produce works of art or, in any case, to carry out an artistic work that really concerns the people. It appeared that works of art were becoming more and more enigmatic for the public, more and more elitist. And that was paradoxical, for it was the time when, in France, the State was using all sorts of means to develop cultural centres and museums. From the other direction, the predominance of the avant-garde movements was disturbing. Their leaders let us think that outside of their way of producing works there was no salvation. To find another position to develop art which would really concern the public seemed to me a necessity.

The American minimalists have influenced you heavily...

What particularly interested me in some American artists was a smoothing out of the trace, of the artist's print, the artist's hand. Contrary to the romantic vision that bestows upon it a surplus of meaning, the minimalists developed the idea that the work can be made by others. They've taken into account industrial production, even if the works' manufacture remained artisanal. A kind of sharing was generated by that attitude. That, for me, seemed to take the artist out of his studio, out of his other-world position. The minimalist's production allowed us to experience less isolation.

And what about Support/Surface?

The deconstruction of the mechanisms of painting carried out by the Support/Surface artists had a critical implication that

Vassivière Arts Center: Reception hall, 1988

Bench (fiberglass), 1989

touched me. Basically it was their questioning about art that interested me, and their works, in that respect, were very explicit. Besides, they seemed to open new aesthetic fields. The work of the Support/Surface group generated a feeling of freedom. But I soon gained the impression that once the mechanisms were dismantled, one didn't get anywhere. That the work became once more a system didn't interest me.

The ambiguity of your relationship with design, in the very way you qualify your work, has been entertained for a long time…

It's the way to talk about it that has entertained that ambiguity. I was constantly reminded of the origins of my work. And if, indeed, my first pieces were sculptural, I soon had as objective to conceive furniture that fit into houses, that fulfilled their role in daily life. It's also possible that the work of some artists whose practice borders on the two disciplines has contributed to maintaining a certain ambiguity. It's equally true that a certain number of preoccupations concerning art can be similar to both disciplines.

Otherness

Your family background, your upbringing, immersed you very early on, in architecture. For you, what are the differences between that discipline and the one of design, both disciplines that contribute to forge our framework of life?

In working on the object I've understood that architecture bore heavier responsibilities than design with regard to the consequences. The architect is, by necessity, more guiding in the organization of life. Once realised, architecture has less flexibility. On the other hand, as a designer one can leave more room for the other – the user–for his own destiny as "creator" of his environment. One can help people be responsible for their framework of life. Architects can do that too, but only in the framework of private commissions, once a close collaboration with the client is established. I think that then, the architect plays an important role vis-à-vis the future user. He has to make him talk, to allow him to find the words that will make the design of his house possible, and to express the way he wishes to live in it. As regards the designer, he proposes a certain number of objects, furniture or operating principles. Insofar as the objects are lighter and already built, the user is going to be able to make that ground work on the objects by himself, in a sense he is going to choose them, and appropriate them as if it was him who had made them. He makes out of the chosen object his thing, as if he had himself discovered it. That relationship of appropriation seems important to me, a reason why I feel as necessity to conceive objects charged with strong and varied signs. Industry has to learn not to always want to clone the same type of objects in vast quantity, with the result that everybody is furnished in the same way, or, anyway, in the same spirit. It seems to me that thanks to new technologies and new tools, one can imagine the existence of differentiated industrial productions. Design must allow us to acknowledge ourselves in our differences and not only in our similarities. There is, at the heart of those preoccupations, an important question for me,

Shelvings (stained wood), Neotu Ed., 1991

that of alterity. That's to say, individuals are singular, their differences are at stake in social games. The objects of daily life allow us to give a meaning, to mark our divergences, our particularities. Today, it seems important to talk about it, to work on that question of alterity faced with that tendency to level everything, reflected in a mondialization, making everything universal, and a rapidity of exchanges. Everything inclines to convince us that we are all perfectly identical.

> *Can one say that the preoccupation with introducing strong signs in the objects, in order to outline their differences, draws you closer to the work of an artist, to the notion of the unique piece?*

What has always captivated me in art is the idea that the work of art allows an exchange between the person who creates it and the person who looks at or appropriates it. There is, if not a communion, at least a very strong link established between them. That relationship interests me. On the other hand, the notion of unique piece is not at all relevant. The mere fact that a piece is unique doesn't automatically place it at the level of a work of art. Its rarity will eventually make it a sought after item. The users are the ones who are unique. And our duty is to allow them to freely organize their close environment with differentiated propositions

Representation

It's also a chair, *conceived in 1982, is your first piece of furniture. Today it appears to me extremely emblematic of your work: already it shows the result of a thorough reflection on proportions, materials, colour. That piece also bears the preoccupations that you've not stopped exploring since: the notion of archetype and the question of absence. Can you talk about the genesis of that piece?*

Designing a chair was obvious, for it is the closest object to the body. It's also an extremely strong object in the sense that it's theatrical: it allows the staging of a space, whatever the space. It is the most mobile furniture. That first piece was at the same time a kind of manifesto to say that I was not an artist.

In that respect, that piece is marked with a certain ambiguity.

It's true. *It's also a chair*, whose title echoes Magritte's, is both the object and its representation. I'd wanted to confront myself with a subject that speaks to the world and, at the same time, is in the world. The chair is both a piece of furniture and a metaphor: it speaks about those who use it. The seat is naturally the trace, the imprint in negative of the person who's going to possess it. To establish that link seems obvious to me. When it's not occupied, the chair is the sign of its potential use. In these terms, in whatever place a group of chairs is, it's at the same time the sign of absence and the mark of those who are going to gather. It is the dramatizing, the staging of life and social relationships. When the chairs are placed around a table, one can see them from behind, they speak about the staging of the meal: they evoke a group of people sitting around the table. That the chairs, placed in front of the table, even when empty, relate to that idea, interests me

Trashcan, installation of the park of the Château of Azay-le-Rideau
ph: Edouard Nono

enormously. A few things, an apparently relatively simple work can refer us to that instant of sharing. For that first piece *It's also a chair*, to be visible as representation, it seemed important to me that it was shifted in relation to the immediate mental image we have of it. The shift was made with a work on proportions: a thickness that's slightly too large, a dimension that's slightly too small. It was not the case of making 'the' chair or the summing up of all chairs. I wanted to find the form which could speak the strongest about the chair.

The question was to get nearer to the archetype of the chair.

It's not so much the idea of the archetype that interests me, rather the idea that an object, whatever it is, must be identifiable, that a given function has to be perceptible. Every change of form modifies the comprehension, the reading and finally the use of the object. I'm opposed to the idea that the couple form/function would become outdated. Everything that composes the object must participate in a readability of the whole. The addition of signs which would make it complex, or even would modify the meaning, are useless. So I undertake a smoothing out of what is superfluous, a kind of tightening that produces an effect of homogeneity. That which calls to your mind the archetype.

Beyond its singular proportions, that chair imposes by its monolithic and smooth appearance.

I didn't want people to see the joins in order to generate a very strong vision of unity. If I had had the opportunity at the time, I would have used a material that could be moulded. As for the colour, faded, it was undoubtedly that which was best to evoke the image of a block. I wanted to achieve that effect of the colour not looking added, but being integrated into the object. That question of unity is even more perceptible in a piece like *Zénith* and can be constantly found in my work, as well as in the pieces made out of resin, for example the round table, the *ABS* chairs, as in my last collection of furniture for Neotu (1997), especially the lounge chair. Besides, I felt deeply the necessity to smooth out everything that could relate strongly to workmanship, the touch, that personal mark. Everything could have been made in an industrial way. The choice of thicknesses, densities, the one of a monochrome colour, the smooth and laquered appearance of the piece had to relate to a manufactured thing like industry can make.

Material, colour and texture

It appears that, work after work, you exploit one material after another. It's also a chair *is made of lacquered wood, a material you used until 1986. After a short parenthesis using galvanized steel, you used MDF, then resin, stained ash, and, in the last collection, textiles and upholstering techniques. What's the idea that presides over the choice of material, and why exploit it alone most of the time?*

A collection often starts with the "idea" of an object, of a production or function. During the development of that "idea", a certain number of questions emerge on the periphery. If the starting point eventually becomes blurred, however, the feeling remains that the final pieces belong to a group. The material perhaps acts as the link between each of the pieces. So for the last collection presented at Neotu, I started working on the designs of the stitches of a sofa in order to bring more density to the volume. Then, I felt like extending that research to other forms that constituted an ensemble. I have none a priori with regard to the materials except that I like to work with materials that can last, whose qualities and characteristics allow me to realize pieces which will age decently, which won't be confined right away to the fashion of the day. The choice of a single material relates to the question of the perception and homogeneity of the object. I like the idea that the object, even if it is made of many pieces, has only one body. Besides, I prefer to establish combinations, tensions, games between objects rather than inside one single object. Beyond, the choice of materials has always been linked for me to given preoccupations. Mass, relationship between form and colour are treated in an obvious way in the lacquered wood pieces. Lacquered wood, like resin, involves a type of fabrication that authorizes more demonstration in the sphere of the form. Resin has also allowed me to deal with the question of relief, the curve and having a formal approach which related to contemporary industrial techniques of moulding and injecting. I wanted to question the modes of fabrication, to be in a formal register which was contemporary and could have been picked up by industry. With wood and textiles I was able to once more find softer and warmer accents. The idea was to choose materials that were best adapted to the project and to use their specific character to give a feeling of formal evidence where nothing can be modified.

Omnipresent in your work, colour is almost always used in monochrome and remains extremely discreet. How does it participate in the creation of a piece?

I don't know exactly how, at a certain point, an obvious relationship is established between a colour and a form. On the other hand, it is clear that colours, which have for the most part dull tones, participate in the density of forms that they cover. The use of a strong green on the *Liliploon*'s chair and the *Epiploon* armchair is one of the rare exceptions to that "rule". Thinking about it, that goes with the fact that these are seats whose shell is like a net. One abandons the range of thickness for that of lightness.

In your work great importance is given to touch. At the same time you used ranges of similar materials for quite a while. What role does the question of touch have?

Touch is what's particular to furniture compared to architecture. Furniture is, by definition, movable: one shifts it, one maintains a strong physical relationship with it. It seems thus of prime necessity to pay attention especially to treatments of the surface. The texture of the lacquered wood pieces originates from a work on lacquer. These have been polished to obtain a certain softness, an effect of warmth. With the resin I used surface grains that appeared to be more complex and rich on contact. The tactile dimension comes into play too in the choice of varieties of wood, textiles, padding materials. But if mastery of the totality of the elements which compose an object interests me, it's in order to come nearer to the right form, the right colour, the right texture, the right proportions, and for everything to participate in the object's unity.

In the human scale

You pay particular attention to the proportions that correspond both to the meaning of the object and also its function. When you started, you didn't contemplate handing over the realization, the moment during which you could still work on the scale. That's no longer the case today.

I don't really hand it over. I take part closely in the making of each of my pieces. More experienced now, I am more precise as to the determination of the relationships between the size and the effect they are going to produce on the object's presence. Forms are always played with in a delicate balance between scale, proportions and slight shiftings which create an unsettling. The relationship to the scale translates in my work through the small displacements giving a certain "accent" to the objects. That particular attention is not the result of some mathematics. I have no modular. It represents the will to shift norms and habits. Aside from established canons, the relationship to proportions that interests me is linked to the human scale in its diversity. Beyond the scale, which is dependent on architecture and corresponds to spaces in which one can enter, there is the scale that relates to what one can embrace, to what one can take into one's arms or hands: the furniture, the objects. Finally, there is the dimension of what one holds in the hand, which is more intimate. The more one goes towards the small dimension, towards intimacy, the more one summons up touching, things further away from the look. That swift classification shows that one goes from a thought that priviliges the visual thing towards a thought that is essentially interested in what is in the tactile field. However the perception of objects passes from one field to the other in complex mixings. That is why I give much attention to the question of proportions: in my opinion it is through that angle that one can best requalify the objects, playing on the variations, the displacement in relation to the conventional norms or dimensions. Slight shiftings allow the creation of confusion. One can thus play on various notions such as comfort, for example, through the sole visual perception.

The meanings of the object

In the catalogue of the exhibition "Vivre en couleur" (Living in colour) (Cartier Foundation, 1985), you explain that at the beginning of each project, you gather notes and sketches while proceeding by idea associations. A kind of putting yourself into a state before starting on the phase of drawing a specific piece. Can you develop that process of creation?

Before drawing a piece, a knife for example, it's obvious that a certain number of ideas are going to pass through my mind, existing objects too like daggers, pocket knives and other blades. To think about drawing the handle is going to evoke certain tools. Connections will take place. Then I shall attempt to integrate that

Loveseat (upholstery), Ed. Neotu, 1991

ensemble of personal references with the idea of the knife that I continually draw, until all those little signs disappear. One returns to the term of archetype, even if it's not exactly right. Anyway, I would like that smoothing out to represent what the object should be. I try to suppress everything that is anecdotal, everything that reduces to concept and idea. Today we live at a time of overvaluation of ideas to the point of putting forward the idea as sufficient reason in the object. I prefer people to have ideas on fundamental questions like justice, how the world should go. Objects are made to be used. One doesn't live with images. If I sit on a chair, I am sitting on a seat, not an idea. Ideas that allow the making of "object-images" generate pieces that wear out quickly. So everything that is not inscribed in an essential way in the objects I work on, I shall have to remove. That's what is at play in the drawing.

> *You wrote: "If an object has been carefully considered, if it is slightly sophisticated, it will make a richer impression on the life of the person who acquires it." Isn't that utopian?*

Every user deserves to be proposed objects that have meaning. Even if it occurs in a more or less intuitive way, this meaning can be linked to the work on form, to the process of manufacture, to the relation with its use and its cultural anchoring. And, undoubtedly, to all of that at the same time. In *L'Empire des Signes*, when Roland Barthes talks about chopsticks, he shows us that very clearly. That's how it is, the relationship one has with objects. The more open one is to seize what they are, the more one is interested in them, the richer they are in meaning.

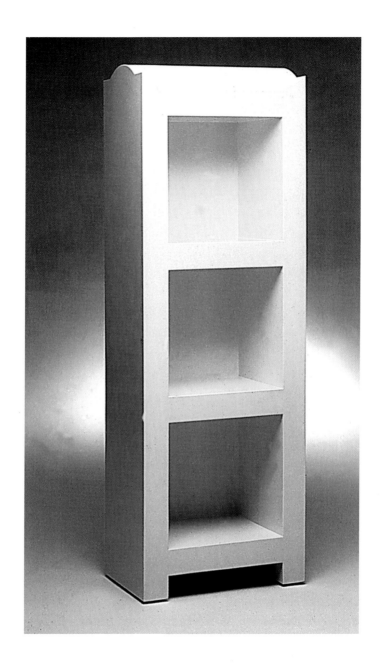

Zenith (lacquered wood), 1982

Most of your pieces are only really finished once they receive a title. And concerning the title, you once said: "it speaks about the objects without ever illustrating them."

The titles combine, before all, to charge the objects with an added meaning. In the gap between the object and its title, a dimension is created in which the imaginary can take place. That allowed me to make a general survey of the object and also allowed the other, the user, to enrich his perception and to appropriate the object more singularly, more individually. The title was a way to speak beside the object, about what had generated the work, about the concerns in the periphery of the objects themselves. *It's also a chair*, which questions the notion of representation, is the counterpart of *Ceci n'est pas une pipe* (This is not a pipe). In its organization, its pot shapes which are multiplied and superimposed, the small piece of furniture *A/rangement* relates to Brancusi and Raynaud. It is an arrangement with sculpture. The use of the privative prefix "A" also brings a contradiction in the title: *A/rangement* is a storage unit, and is not entirely that. *Zénith* whose form allows a rigorous verticality, alludes to the stature of a standing man and refers also to the light, to the colour of the day when the sun is at its highest. Beyond the question of meaning, it seems to me that the title was also a way to name objects that didn't belong to the usual typologies of furniture. On the other hand, in the series of "addressed forms", the stake was the identification of the persons to whom the pieces were destined, rather than the designation of the pieces of furniture themselves. In that collection, the writing desk *Je vous souhaite le bonjour mon cher Roland* (I wish you a good morning my dear Roland) is a grey piece of furniture which one bumps into, as is the case with some monastic writing desks whose working surface is sloped and before which one adopts a sitting/standing position. While I was working on that piece a text came into my hands on the difficulty of writing, on the alertness necessary for that task. That text had the peculiarity of being constructed as a letter the author addressed to himself. The title for the writing desk is taken from the first words. Those different examples show how the composition of a title is each time singular and can appear enigmatic. It's the result of a little story, and the day when the user discovers it he can experience an added sensation. At the same time, it is also possible that he won't know it. Today, recourse to a title as a way of communicating no longer seems necessary. The pieces are more obvious, more easily identified, they are self-sufficient. That doesn't prevent them sometimes bearing the name of their sleeping partners: it's a sign of affection and I like to remember who's at the origin of them.

The edition

Since 1985, and the first collective exhibition, your furniture has been regularly shown in the Neotu gallery, where you have presented five collections. What influence does that close collaboration with a gallery owner have on your work?

That collaboration has interfered a lot in the way I've conducted my work. In the early 1980s, I didn't have any plans to be a designer. I was in the midst of questioning my activity while

Square table (stained medium density fiberboard), Cartier Foundation, 1985

around me others spoke about the death of art. At that time I met a lot of people, amongst them Pierre Staudenmeyer and Gérard Dalmon from the Neotu Gallery. They were quick to propose a collective exhibition for me to take part in, followed by my first personal exhibition. That relationship I maintained with the Neotu Gallery was interesting. I wanted it to develop. Little by little we've started a true collaboration based on trust and respect. It was, and still is, a marginal situation in relation to the reality of the big houses. Nevertheless, at the beginning of the 1980s, at the time when I began to make furniture, Neotu was, in France, the only place for possible dialogue, with, equally, the VIA. Those spaces had an identical aim, to "rekindle" furniture design in France, to restore its vitality and meaning.

Beyond the role of agent and editor, has Pierre Staudenmeyer, with whom you've become friends, played a role as privileged interlocutor?

When I prepare a collection, we don't really talk about it. But as for Pierre or his partner Gérard Dalmon, before he left to direct Neotu New York, they've always understood what I engage in my work. They respect it and trust me by allowing me to move forward. It's a real chance. I had, and still have, thanks to Neotu, the possibility and freedom to begin a personal reflection knowing that the gallery is going to regularly give me an exhibition that will permit me to take stock of the state of my work. As for the question of production, Neotu has, since the beginning, developed the structure of a limited edition. My collections have earned the right to exist thanks to the gallery, even if today I'd prefer that they

Stool from the "Tropic collection", 1992

had been more widely distributed. One would've thought that after an experimental phase, there would be a development and an opening in another type of edition. I thought it was possible. But I haven't looked elsewhere. The continuous collaboration with Neotu has positioned me in a singular way. I assume entire responsibility. One shouldn't forget that Neotu remains a place for investigation, for research, with the role of discoverer and editor in an exceptional framework.

What impact had the 'standing invite' of the VIA in 1983?

The VIA structure was young, me too. I continued to work solo.

You gave the impression of not having cared about the distribution of your pieces.

To make the move, to go and look for editors, that's something I can't do. Beyond that certain lack, a moral dimension comes into play in the exercise of this profession. Futility, the throwaway nature of things annoys me. For me it's an old attitude, that of not wanting to waste. And that makes sense today. Everything that relates to fast consumption has no other result than to clutter our environment. That ecological preoccupation is obviously a concern common to all of us as individuals. Naturally it forms the backdrop of my practice. There is a huge difference between a designer who's conscious of human problems and one who pretends to resolve them with design.

The tropical collection

You took part, with Martine Bedin and Eric Joudan, in a project initiated by T.N. Tchakaloff, director of the Maison française du meuble créole in La Réunion, which resulted in "The tropical collection". That project represents a singular experience for a designer since the question is to explore a foreign culture, local know-how, in order to imagine furniture which could be realised on the spot and would form a kind of register of shapes for the island's crafts people. How did it take place?

"The tropical collection" remains a fascinating and exceptional adventure. First the meeting with Tchakaloff, a man who loves furniture, then the discovery of the place and its history. We arrived on the island of Réunion without any preconceived ideas, and started by observing the traditions, the culture, the local know-how. In particular we brought back to light rich and complex practices derived from cultural criss-crossings that happened on an island situated at the intersection of the ways between Asia and Europe. Perhaps we were able, as outsiders, to bring a fresh look. Nothing would have been possible without much listening and an even greater respect for the practices and know-how of the crafts people as well as for past influences. That's perhaps the reason why the most successful pieces of the collection are those that are furthermost in relation to our usual stylistic treatments, to our respective signatures. Insofar as the local industry is relatively limited and somehow slightly different than

Chair *ABS 1*, Neotu Ed., 1993

the one found in the metropolis, it was necessary to conform to the tools used on the spot and see that the evolutions were the gentlest possible. It was a case of showing that the artisanal production could be developed, could still be resourceful. Rather than giving models to be repeated ad infinitum, our role consisted in underlining that it was still possible to make the situation evolve. The most interesting part of that project was to allow us to think about the type of furniture made on the island with regard to the production which comes from Europe, and to make new propositions with the idea that they had to go beyond us, not to belong to us any longer.

How was the collection built?

First came the question of determining what was the most legitimate framework for our intervention. We chose the verandah, the transitory living space between interior and exterior, a place for discussions, a place to rest. It's the spot of the house on the outside, a controlled exterior. Then we decided the typology of the furniture. We thought about the types of rooms we could question regarding the space of the verandah in order to finally release fifteen or so objects that we virtually choses at random! The objects I drew come from around the table. The use of African wood varieties – which are the closest to those that could be found on the island – and a caning in cane fibres characterize the ensemble. The manufacturing process which allows use of the same tools for the realization of each piece of the furniture also produces a form that connects one to the other. The choice of caning was obvious insofar as it is the object of a true culture in the

Réunion. Besides, caning, with its loose weaving, offers maximum aeration, an essential element in a tropical country. That solution is even more ideal because the fibre, by remaining constantly moistened, is resistant and doesn't wear out. Beyond its practical aspect, the material interested me in the production which generates the pattern: how, in weaving the fibre in a regular way, does one succeed in creating a woof and weft? After having chosen the most refined caning model, I "fiddled" with it to modify just slightly its pattern. Caning always has a pattern, it's inescapable. I wanted to draw it again to be sure it was structured. Everything has to be drawn again and again very carefully so that nothing is left to chance. That doesn't necessarily show. One can think it's a fairly common caning but if one looks closer, one notices a sparer drawing. That shift identifies the object. Changing the perception of an object slightly interests me, making an intervention at a spot where nobody expects it. It's not a matter of change for the sake of change, but rather of giving back density and strength by exacerbating the signs of construction, giving them back body. In the case of caning, I wondered about a way to make the pattern more visible, to affirm the aesthetic.

Has "The tropical collection", as a singular experience, had a particular impact on your following work?

Obviously, I learnt a lot during that project. It has undoubtedly nourished and enriched my writing and my vocabulary. But in continuity: my preoccupations haven't changed for all that. Changing from one work to another, there are zones of resonance conditioned by the successive experiences. Some aspects are toned

Daybed (upholstery), Neotu Ed., 1997

down, others are revealed or displaced. That's visible in the forms, the organization of the objects or the choice of materials.

From furniture to the 'table arts'

You approached design through furniture. Today, without abandoning that typology, you turn your attention to the table arts. It appears to be an old concern of yours – I think about a project of table service for the Manufacture de Giens. What is your interest in returning to those preoccupations with the table arts?

The furniture as I've engaged it through the collections shown at Neotu, or through particular commissions, as well as the table arts, deal with the physical as well as visual relationship one maintains with the material world. The preoccupations which underlie my work stay the same, except that the physical relationship with a small object doesn't concern the whole body any longer, but only the hand. In the table service projects I'm currently conducting, I'm mainly interested in the question of touch, the sensations and information it gives back to us. Still that preoccupation is about the framework of life. I see, I touch and I organize the world with objects I chose for their sensorial as well as the symbolic qualities I maintain with them. That the essential part of my work is turned towards domestic space sounds right to me, insofar as the framework of intimate life is concerned. This also echoes a concern for the other and relates to the question of proximity with the user. Without excluding public space, nevertheless the house appears to be the privileged place to question the relationship to the other.

You have now approached the table arts in the framework of the "Vallauris project", initiated in 1998 by the city and the Ministry of Culture, and which aims at valorizing a local know-how.

I chose to develop a work on moulding and the technique of casting to make the pieces relatively easy to make, the most faithful possible to the project, the most economical in manufacturing and the most identifiable as objects coming from the Vallauris production. It was an implicit rule to propose objects which reflect the local production insofar as each designer was asked to work on the spot in collaboration with a craftsperson of their choice, in my case it was Gabriel Musarra. I took my inspiration from local tradition, whether for the choice of objects (the tea and coffee set), choice of technique (casting is one of the great practices of the region), or for the colour, that peculiar yellow which was in fashion in the 1950s, Vallauris' golden age. Handling the moulding led me to play on the levels of joint, the seams of its two parts. This allowed me to make the manufacturing of the pieces readable. Their shape itself, as well as the strong presence of the seams, indicate clearly the use of casting. Besides, the moulding of pieces allows an economy on fettling at the end of the process, as well as an economy in the manufacturing, insofar as each object is made of one single piece. I sought to keep with the most simplified manufacturing process.

Today you pursue that exploration of the table arts with a free hand from the VIA which should be presented in January 2001. What are you work directions?

The VIA wished to give me a free hand in the table arts when it was proposed to me. That perspective seduced me immediately for it seems that the question of the relationship between the tactile and visual dimensions of the objects, of the physical relationship that one maintains with them, is tightly played in that typology of products. When we eat, all the actions that summon touch – to grasp the cutlery, to seize the plate, to break bread – firmly contribute to forge our sensorial images, in other words, the way we perceive the world. Today we know that these images are created from a complex organization which summon up the whole of our senses. To approach the table service is an opportunity to attempt a synthetic work which calls on the five senses. It's not so far from what I usually do. So working on table service and cutlery sends us back to the question of the staging of the framework of life, of the scale. For the moment my research is made in an intuitive way. I meet specialists as diverse as neurologists and chefs who help me to understand how all my preoccupations, which turn around food, its presentation, the objects that help to dress the table, function and are articulated in our global perception of a meal.

Interior/Exterior

When you create furniture, while stipulating your own specifications, you never intend it for a specific place. How, in this case, do you approach a commission for an interior development?

The main question concerns not so much the place as the people who live in it. The place is obviously of some importance in the sense that one has to respect it. But as much as I can, I try to make propositions which are the lightest and most mobile as possible. What is at stake is as always, the user. How is he going to appropriate the furniture in the space that is imparted to him?

Do you imagine a scenario? Do you meet the people who'll live in the space you're going to work on?

I cannot do without meeting the future users. Their approval is necessary. My first development, the offices of the Fondation Cartier in Jouy-en-Josas, was born of a relationship of complicity with Marie-Claude Beaud, director of the institution at the time. Facing her project and the organization of her team's work, I initiated a dialogue with all the people concerned around the idea of simple and economical furniture which permits the biggest number of possible combinations. These exchanges lead me to imagine a very diversified development where everyone could organize and personalize his working place according to his own needs. To reinforce the differences, we also varied the coloured ambiances of each office. I liked that project a lot, likewise the Vassivières' one. The Art Centre is a wonderful space. Aldo Rossi knew how to conceive an architecture which was both strong and open. To furnish the reception hall, I created furniture made of red tinted wood, light and mobile, which plays in contrast with the granite building. The Vassivières experience is the exact opposite of that of the Jeu de Paume Museum where I was given the job of developing the café. The plan here was linked to an architecture that was completely enclosed and allowed little freedom of action. But whatever the commission, my main preoccupations concern the definition of the programme. The main directions appear while specifying the programme as best one can with the future users. Less directive, more subtle solutions emerge that way. The designer's role is to determine a certain number of mobile objects which are going to participate in the ambiance of the place. The ambiance remains after all the prerogative of the people who inhabit it. I think one cannot fix in a definite way the theatralization of a living or working place. One can bring in a certain number of elements which will bestow a tone, a colour, particular and specific accents. But the framework of life cannot be fixed by some outsider. I like the idea that everyone of us is responsible for his own living space. It belongs to us, the designers, to propose objects and furniture that are sufficiently interesting.

You have carried out various studies on urban furniture – inter-district connections in Dunkerque, a furniture project in Saint-Etienne – and peri-urbans. You now pursue the development of the park of the château at Azay-le-Rideau. How does that confrontation with the landscape and its scale unfold?

Whenever it concerns interventions in urban or rural milieu, I obviously work on the relationship between furniture and landscape. The role of the furniture is the same everywhere: thanks

to it we can punctuate and put rhythm into spaces while underlining
the various relationships of scale. Let's take, for example, the
furniture project for the Bourriane parks. I proposed very simple
tables and seats for the exterior, similar to the ones you can see
everywhere in the countryside, in this type of park. The specificity
of this project is linked to the will to make those spaces more clear,
neater, and that comes from the simple fact that, under the benches,
feet dig little holes and the grass disappears, leaving a dirt patch. I
thought to place the furniture on concrete paving stones as if it was
placed on carpets thrown onto the landscape. And there a
voluntarily marked relationship is established: the "carpets" give
rhythm and punctuate the landscape. But, before all, I think about
the quality of the relationship between user and objects. We are still
concerned by the same questions of identifying the objects,
recognizing them, appropriating them, developing with them a
singular relationship. In Azay-le-Rideau, I wanted to integrate the
furniture into the landscape and play on contrasts betweeen scales.
What's interesting is to see what reaction is generated by a dustbin
whose diameter is going to be more or less equivalent to that of a
tree trunk, whose tree is some thirty times higher. The relationship
of scale between these elements will not only be very strong but will
play on the perception we have of the landscape. In the same way if
one places a bench under full-grown trees, suddenly, the scale of the
trees takes its own dimension. There is thus a reading of the
landscape which is induced by the furniture itself. The furniture
becomes a referent element. One qualifies the space with the
furniture one installs. That it concerns the park of a château has no
particular implication. Vigilance, attention, respect of the place in

which one is have to be identical everywhere. On the other hand, writing will be different according to the space. In Azay-le-Rideau I picked up again, for the first drawings of the benches, the horizontal lines which echoed the barriers and fences of the surrounding fields. After that I developed for all the cast iron furniture little signs inspired by images of lattice works and willow leaves which relate more to the image of a historic park than to the park of a château. I also worked on the descriptive supports destined to welcome with information on the history of the park and on the plant life present. In this case it was necessary to conceive a form both discreet and in relation to the other furniture. I used cast iron again and carried out a formal work in the background: they are objects one must hardly see apart from the information they carry. The development project finally comprises a footbridge and a folly. These two works need to receive, engraved on their handrails, additional indications on the fauna and flora. Their vocation is to increase interest in the park by accompanying the walk of the visitors, by seeing to it that the public walks away from the château in an affable and comfortable framework. The ensemble of the furniture participates with the folly as focal point.

The affective quality of the objects

In 1985 you wrote: "I think the designer is not in anyway the bearer of a message." What is your position today as a designer?

I think about the extraordinary term of "creator" in which they dressed us during the eighties. As if we were in possession of some kind of truth. And I think about the way the designer's work today is valued, by presenting them as people who have sufficient authority to plan, on their own, tomorrow's world. One mustn't give too much attention to that sort of talk. Like all designers I participate through the conception of objects in the creation of our environment. And, as such, I commit my responsibility. It is no more serious than that, one is not going to change the world, only trying to make it a better place. That said, there are different ways to exercise the profession of designer. The taking into account of technological progress, which results in one conceiving and making better and better all kinds of objects which become more reliable and more economical, is an important dimension of design. Another way to think about design also exists today, which is close to some practices in contemporary art. One questions the capacities of the informative tool to form objects. One conceives the fabrication of the object as demonstration in relation to the techniques. And, by themselves, these questions are enough to make sense. That doesn't satisfy me. One doesn't live with things that are demonstrations, with logical organizations that would signify the making of the world. Beyond their practical existence, their material reality, objects accompany us in life. They are inscribed in a story, in a culture. They are vectors of exchange, but also of transmission, for they appear and disappear in a time different from ours. They represent our time and at the same time, survive it. Objects qualify us and we are visible through them, we represent ourselves through them. That articulation poses a certain number of questions which turn around appropriation, resemblance and the affective dimension of the objects. These are at the heart of my preoccupations. If I make furniture it is for the people. What interests me is that the furniture could resemble them. Each individual has the opportunity, the intelligence, to be able to participate in his own framework of life, to choose what corresponds to him. The border is quickly crossed from lucidity to fabricate one's domestic world from all the possibilities, in consideration of one's own needs to identification with objects and resemblance. I choose things that are going to represent me, in which I am going to feel good, to feel myself. The objects are in a way a reflection of myself when an exactness between desires, aspirations and needs takes place.

Do you feel close to the movement termed by the press as "minimalist"?

As much as I feel close to the American artistic movement, so as much I don't fit absolutely into the course of design. That particular minimalism was a way to draw towards dematerialization. Now I am in the form, not in the absence of form, despite the smoothing out I systematically carry out.

The border is thin between smoothing out and absence of form.

In the first place, one doesn't follow the same processes of thought, the same course of research. With "minimalism", a term that incidentally appears very exaggerated, one insinuates that the objects would have less weight in the future, less presence and would leave room for a dematerialization of the material world. As for me, I think that, on the contrary, we need objects firmly set in our culture, our memory, which carry meaning. The smoothing out of the superfluous, the anecdotal, the image goes in the direction of a search for roots.

Teaching

Parallel to your activity as a designer, you've always taught. In your experience, what does that parallel activity bring you – contact with students?

When I started to teach, I thought it was possible to transmit knowledge, ideas, to imagine a pedagogy. It seemed to me that in that free space that is a school, teachers could make things move in relation to accepted ideas. Today, with experience, I think that it's a delusion to have an opinion in relation to teaching. Teachers are simply there in order that the "school" structure exists. Then, exchanges with students relate to the sponge game which operates, of course, in a reciprocal way.

From the outside, one thinks that a school of Saint-Etienne design exists. And that apparently has a lot to do with you.

It's a common school phenomenon. When a few designers teach at the heart of an establishment, it's obvious they are going to leave their marks. We're back to the sponge game which also plays a role in the profession. So, rapprochements between my work and the work of other designers are possible. But if I have a so-called influence for two decades, it operates above all through small touches and relates to the fact that I participate in an epoch, in an ensemble movement.

The global vision of your journey shows a strong coherence both in the formal rigour which lasts and in a typological rigour. At the same time your work seems to reflect an evolution towards more softness. It's striking in your last collection shown at the Neotu gallery. One recognizes the massive forms of your first works but more curved, more generous, more "languid".

I notice that my concerns are often of the same order. I think that the harder, sparer aspect of my first pieces is probably linked to the necessity to mark a territory and to have consequently, a demonstrative work. I had to overdo it a bit. With time, that necessity to produce pieces which discourse has blurred, has disappeared. Besides, I believe that my questioning today is more discreet, more open and concerns more minute things. It's true it can appear modest. The question is not to turn everything upside down but rather to talk about our daily life, about our relationship to the objects. I have the feeling that by constantly working on those apparently common questions, one succeeds in touching the very essence of things.

Colour pictures index

1: *Téranice 3*, bench (galvanized steel),1983

2: *Family Chairs*, 1992

3: *Alligator*, yellow chair (lacquered wood), 1984

4: Grey writing desk and yellow chair (lacquered wood), 1984

5: *Epiploon* chair (fiberglass), 1983

6: Daybed (fiberglass and tennis court flooring), 1986

7: Table (fiberglass on cardboard), 1989

8: Ivory *Female* chair (fiberglass), Neotu Ed., 1993

9: Ivory *Male* chair (fiberglass), Neotu Ed., 1993

10: Chair (fiberglass), Neotu Ed., 1991

11: Tall portico (lacquered wood), 1989

12: Container (double access, fiberglass), 1989

13: Round table (fiberglass), Neotu Ed., 1991

14: Centerpiece (bronze), Neotu Ed., 1991

15: National Prizes Trophy (molded glass), 1988

16: CIRVA vase (molded glass), 1988

17: Writing desk (stained wood), Neotu Ed., 1991

18: Canning (detail). "Tropic collection", 1992

19: Bench. "Tropic Collection", 1992

20: "Tropic collection", 1992

21: "Ears" chair (upholstery), Neotu Ed. , 1997

22: *La vie en rose* vase, pottery, Cartier Foundation, 1998

23: *Studio* table, 1996

24: Bookcase (touka wood), Neotu Ed., 1997

25: Coffee and tea vessels, pottery, "Vallauris collection" (detail), 1999

26: Coffee and tea vessels, pottery, "Vallauris collection", Artcodif Ed., 1999

27: *Françoise*, vase "Vallauris collection", Neotu Ed., 1999

▼ 1

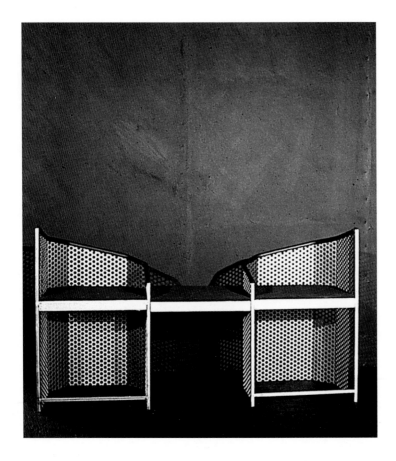

5 ▶

6 ▶

▲ 10 ▲ 11

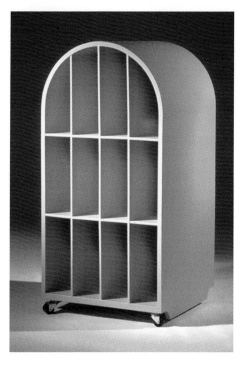

◀ 12

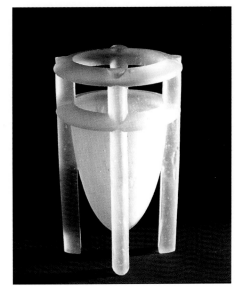

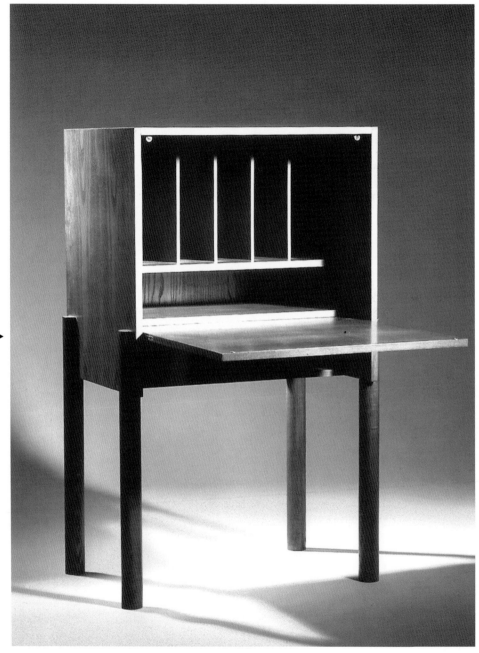

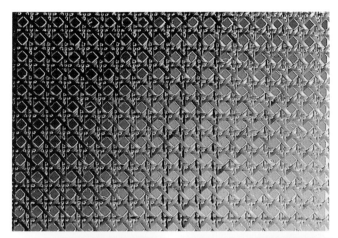

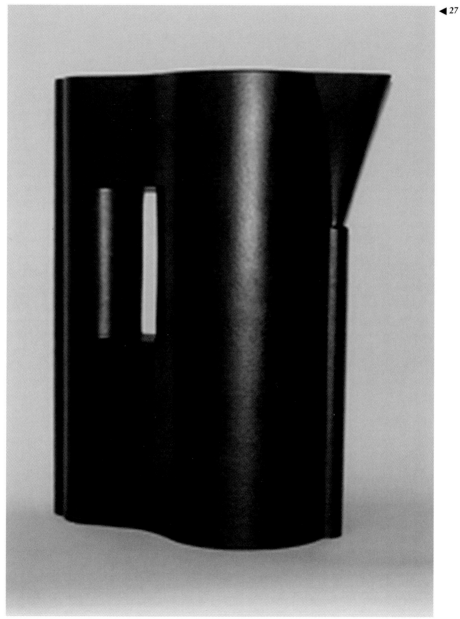

Biography

1948
Born in Montluçon, France

1970-1975
Student at the Bourges Art School

1978-1982
Professor at the Mâcon Art School
Since 1982, professor at the Saint-Etienne
Art School

1981
Design of the first lacquered wood pieces
of furniture: *It's also a chair*, *Vanity*,
Zenith, and *A/rangement*

1982
It's also a chair, coffered and lacquered
plywood, granted a standing invitation by
the VIA
During this period, François Bauchet
designed lacquered wood furniture.

1983
Creation of steel furniture, development
of the *Téranice* line in punched and folded
galvanized steel

1985
François   Bauchet   meets   Pierre
Staudenmeyer and Gérard Dalmon and
begins his collaboration with the Neotu
gallery where his works are permanently
presented. Every two years, a new
collection is presented

1985-1987
Devoted Forms, lacquered wood

1987-1989
Creation of a series of composite crafted
pieces in fiberglass on cardboard

1989-1991
Development of more functional pieces of
furniture: bookcases, writing desk, stained
wood tables, presented at the Neotu
gallery in 1991

1993
Presentation of a chair collection, Neotu,
Paris

1997
Lounge furniture, set of upholstered
furniture

At the present time, François Bauchet is
working on the making of a footbridge
and a folly for the park of the Château of
Azay-le-Rideau. As part of the VIA carte
blanche, he is engaged in research on
Tableware
His works are presented in France at the
Frac (Nord-Pas de Calais), Frac (Rhône
Alpes), The National Fund for Contem-
porary Art, the Museum of Decorative
Arts, (Paris), Design Museum, (Thessa-
loniki, Greece), Museo do design
(Lisbon, Portugal)

Creations

1981

Creation of the first lacquered wood pieces of furniture: *It's also a chair, Zenith Vanity*

1982

VIA, Scholarship: galvanized steel seats

1983

Téranice line (punched steel)

1985

Liliploon chair and *Epiploon* armchair (fiberglass)

1987

Cartier Foundation, Jouy-en-Josas: installation of the office space, creation of a set of furniture and desk accessories
Zeus-Desco, Milan: single-person table and chair (fiberglass)
Spinler, Romans: set of cardboard shelves and console
Neotu, *Devoted Forms*

1988

CIRVA, "Double Transparency": iris vase (molded glass)
Yamagiwa corporation "In-spiration": wall lights
Vassivière-en-Limousin arts center: windows, tables and furniture of the reception hall

1989

Saint-Etienne Museum of Art and Industry: installation of the reception hall (floor, benches, chandeliers and door handles)
Neotu, Paris, storage units and composites collection: container (double access, fiberglass), small and tall portico (lacquered wood), cabinet (birch wood), writing desk, table (fiberglass and cardboard), bench (fiberglass)

1990

National Prizes: molded glass trophy
CIRVA, Marseille Water Board: water carafe
Napoli, French Institute "Design a confronto": postcards box
Neotu New York "New bronze": centerpiece

1991

Neotu: stained wood collection (writing desk, one way and double way shelving, coffee table)

1992

French Company of Creole Furniture: "Tropic Collection" (bench, armchair, stool, flowerpot holder)

"Family Chairs": set of chairs, to combine from twenty cut in molded plywood shells

City of Dunkerque "Du jeu de mail à la basse ville" (From Pall-Mall to down town) a study on inter-districts connections

Galerie du Jeu de Paume/Museum of Contemporary Art: benches of the exhibition rooms, chairs, tables and benches of the café

Kerguéhennec Art Center: exhibition furniture

Neotu: fiberglass pieces (chair 1 and 2, armchair)

Pierre Gagnaire restaurant: tables and cheeseboards, cigars cellar, bench

1993

Neotu: "Chairs", seats collection (pair of ivory fiberglass chairs, *Male* and *Female*, peer wood chair, tall-backed low armchair and sofa, three models of ABS chairs and benches)

1995

French Consulate in Rio de Janeiro: "Brazil", a study on a collection of furniture with the help of the AFAA

City of Saint-Etienne: Mayor's office installation (armchair, sofa, ashtray, mail basket), in collaboration with E. Jourdan

1996

Château of Azay-le-Rideau: park's installation (benches, trashcan, descriptive cards), produced by the National Fund for Historic Monuments and Sites

Saint-Etienne Art School, artists' studio installation: set of metal and plywood pieces (bed, closet, table)

1997

Neotu: lounge furniture, set of upholstered pieces (ottoman, daybed, small sofa, "ears" armchair) and makoré wood furniture (round coffee table, bookcase, jam cupboard)

1998

Cartier Foundation: *La vie en rose* vase (china)

1999

Artcodif, "Vallauris Collection": coffee and tea vessels

Neotu, "Vallauris Collection": *Dominique* vase and centerpiece

2000

Tarkett Sommer: "Private Collection" (random-combinations slabs)

Exhibitions (selection)

1982
Grand boulevard, Bourges

1983
Salon des Artistes décorateurs, VIA

1985
« Jeunes créateurs » («Young creators»),
Autrement, Paris

1986
BDX gallery, Bordeaux
Artérieur gallery, Berlin

1987
« Desco : Tables de célibataires »,
Zeus, Milan
« Documenta 8 », Kassel
Zeus, Milan
Neotu gallery, Paris

1988
« Inspiration », Tokyo, Paris, Milan
« M.D.F. » (Medium Density Fiberboad),
Cartier Foundation, Jouy-en-Josas

1989
« La Double transparence » («Double
transparency»), CIRVA
Neotu gallery, Paris

1990
« Design a confronto », Napoli French
Institute
« Les années VIA » Museum of Decorative
Arts, Paris

1991
« CIRVA, le verre manière de faire »,
Costrie, Saint-Etienne
« Vivre plastique », 2d design quadrennial,
Museum of Art and Industry, Saint-
Etienne
Neotu Gallery, Paris

1993
Neotu Gallery, Paris

1994
« CIRVA, le verre manière de faire »,
Seoul Cultural Center, Korea

1997
« L'art du mobilier en France 1987-1997 »,
Boulogne-Billancourt
 Neotu Gallery, Paris

1998
Galerie Olivier Wieshoff, Brême
« La vie en rose », Cartier Foundation,
Paris

1999
« Collection Vallauris », Vallauris
« Passagen », Reckermann Gallery, Kölhn

Bibliography (selection)

Jean-Claude Conesa, « Suzanne est au salon », exhibition catalogue *À bruit secret*, Dunkerque, 1985

Jacques Bonnot, « Une chaise est une chaise », L'atelier des métiers d'arts, n°101, September 1985

Hubert Besacier, « Vivre en couleur », exhibition catalogue Cartier Foudation, October 1985

Jacques Beauffet, Hubert Besacier, « Formes adressées », A Priori, 1987

Élisabeth Vedrenne, « Fauteuils et canapés », Les carnets du design, n°3, 1987

Chistine Colin, « L'œuvre manquante », Galerie Magazine, n°17, February-March 1987

« Desco », exhibition catalogue, Zeus, Milan, September-October 1987

Hervé Audouard, exhibition catalogue « Meubles d'époque », Théâtre d'Hérouville, Caen, November1987

Documenta 8, Kassel, 1987, Weber & Weidemayer Gmb H & Co

Hubert Besacier, Tandem Industrie-Création, Romans,1987

Claire Peillod, interview, Halle Sud, n°17, October 1988

« In-Spiration », exhibition catalogue, Tokyo-Paris-Milan, 1988

Christine Colin, « Design aujourd'hui », Flammarion,1988

« 30 vases pour le CIRVA », Michel Aveline editor/CIRVA,1989

« Les années VIA », Museum of Decorative Arts, 1990

François Barré, « Du jeu de mail à la basse ville », Dunkerque, Fall 1991

 « Collection Tropicale », october 1992

Claire Fayolle, « État de chaises », Archicréé, n°254, 1993

Chantal Hamaide, « Chaises en vue », Intramuros, n°48, May-June 1993

Pierre Staudenmeyer, « Cahiers de la Serre », n°45, exhibition catalogue, Saint-Etienne, 1996

« Dictionnaire international des arts appliqués et du design », Édition du Regard, 1996

Élisabeth Vedrenne, « Rondeurs et couleurs », L'œil, n°490, November1997

Sophie Roulet, « Création dans les parcs historiques », Archicréé, n°283, 1998

Sophie Tasmas Annargyros, « Portrait », Intramuros, n°75,March 1998

« The International Design Yearbook », Calman & King,1999

« Luxo, pop & cool », Francisco Capelo collection, Design Museum, Lisbon, 1999

Enzo Biffi Gentili, « Utile, Inutile, Outil », Vallauris Collection, June 1999

« CIRVA, le verre manière de faire », Seoul Cultural Center, Korea

Also available from Dis Voir

CINEMA

Jean-Pierre Rehm, Olivier Joyard,
Danièle Rivière
Tsai Ming-liang

Jean-Marc Lalanne, Ackbar Abbas,
David Martinez, Jimmy Ngai
Wong Kar-wai

Paul Virilio, Carole Desbarats,
Jacinto Lageira, Danièle Rivière
Atom Egoyan

Michael Nyman, Daniel Caux, Michel Field,
Florence de Mèredieu, Philippe Pilard
Peter Greenaway

Christine Buci-Glucksmann,
Fabrice Revault d'Allonnes
Raoul Ruiz

Yann Lardeau, Jacques Parsi,
Philippe Tancelin
Manoel de Oliveira

CHOREOGRAPHY

Paul Virilio, René Thom, Laurence Louppe,
Jean-Noël Laurenti,
Valérie Preston-Dunlop
Traces of Dance
Drawings and Notations of Choreographers

ARCHITECTURE

Christian de Portzamparc
Genealogy of forms

DESIGN

Jacques Bonnaval, Claire Fayolle
François Bauchet

Philippe Pernodet, Bruce Mehly
Luigi Colani

Pascale Cassagnau, Christophe Pillet
Starck's Kids ?
(Beef, Matali Crasset,
Jean-Marie Massaud,
Patrick Jouin, Bretillot/Valette)

Chloé Braunstein, Gilles de Bure
Roger Tallon

Charles-Arthur Boyer, Federica Zanco
Jasper Morrison

Pierre Staudenmeyer, Nadia Croquet,
Laurent Le Bon
Garouste et Bonetti

Philippe Louguet, Dagmar Sedlickà
Borek Sìpek

Raymond Guidot, Olivier Boissière
Ron Arad

François Burkhardt, Cristina Morozzi
Andrea Branzi

ÉDITIONS DIS VOIR: 3, RUE BEAUTREILLIS – F-75004 PARIS
TEL (33/1) 48 87 07 09 – FAX (33/1) 48 87 07 14 – EMAIL: DISVOIR@AOL. COM